Holiday Greetings
to Clair from Jackie

OHIO

SMITHMARK

This edition first published in 1992 by SMITHMARK
Publishers Inc., 112 Madison Avenue,
New York, New York 10016

ISBN 0-8317-0510-8

Printed and bound in Spain

Writer: Irene S. Korn
Designer: Ann-Louise Lipman
Design Concept: Lesley Ehlers
Editor: Sara Colacurto
Production: Valerie Zars
Photo Researcher: Edward Douglas
Assistant Photo Researcher: Robert V. Hale
Editorial Assistant: Carol Raguso

Title page: With a span of 1,000 feet,
the John A. Roebling Suspension Bridge
was the longest such bridge in the world
when completed in 1867. The first bridge
to cross the Ohio River, linking Cincinnati
with Kentucky, it is considered the
prototype for Roebling's Brooklyn
Bridge. *Opposite:* The Tyler Davidson
Fountain is the centerpiece of downtown
Cincinnati's Fountain Square. The water
flowing from the maiden's outstretched
hands symbolizes the significance of the
Ohio River to the city.

TO THE
PEOPLE OF
CINCINNATI

This red-brick music hall is home of the Cincinnati Symphony Orchestra, the Cincinnati Ballet, and the Cincinnati Opera Company, the second oldest in the United States. *Below:* George Sugarman's painted aluminum "Cincinnati Story" sculpture and fountain leaves plenty of room for personal interpretation. The twin towers in the background are only a part of Proctor and Gamble's international headquarters.

The spirit of Ohio is probably best summed up by the state's motto: "With God, all things are possible." Although Ohio didn't become a state until 1803, thousands of people moved to the area from the already crowded Eastern seaboard between 1788 and 1789. They came to this part of the Northwest Territory armed only with optimism and a willingness to work hard to make life better for themselves—and they succeeded. Ohio has consistently given birth to people who have changed the United States and the people who live here. People started calling Ohio the "mother of presidents" in the nineteenth century, when three U.S. presidents in a row came from there: Ulysses S. Grant, Rutherford B. Hayes, and James A. Garfield. Although Virginia and Ohio still fight over who can claim William Henry Harrison—who was born in Virginia but moved to Ohio at a young age—they can both agree that he was the person responsible for popularizing the nickname "The Buckeye State" with a series of slogans and songs during his presidential campaign in the mid-1800's. Presidents Benjamin Harrison, William McKinley, William H. Taft, and Warren G. Harding also came from Ohio. Another nickname for the state is "the mother of inventors," Ohio being home to such innovative people as Orville and Wilbur Wright,

The ins and outs of Cincinnati's history: The Museum Center at Union Terminal (top) houses the Museum of Natural History and the Cincinnati Historical Society. The rotunda in the restored Union Terminal is one of the finest examples of Art Deco architecture. Along the streets of downtown, remnants of the city's rich history illuminate signs of the twentieth century (right).

Above: The 1820 Federal-style Taft Museum, former residence of Charles (older half-brother of President William Howard Taft) and Anna Taft, houses the family collection of Chinese porcelain, French enamelware, and paintings by masters such as Goya, Rembrandt, and Whistler. *Below:* The grand scale of the exterior of Cincinnati's City Hall (left) is echoed in the interior with stately marble staircases, high ceilings, and a regal council chamber. Two interior courtyards allow sunlight to play off the stained-glass windows depicting scenes from Ohio's history. From a small company selling candles and soaps, Proctor & Gamble (right) has grown into one of the city's largest employers.

who spent their early years in Dayton trying to perfect their flying machine; Thomas Edison, who gave us the electric light and phonograph, among other inventions; James Ritty, the inventor of the cash register; and Garrett Morgan, who, after seeing a young girl get hit by a car, devised an electric stop sign to help prevent such accidents in the future.

Other natives changed the world in previously undreamed-of ways: Carl Stokes was the first black mayor of a major city (Cleveland); Dr. George Washington Crile performed the first blood transfusion; John Glenn was the first American to orbit the earth; and Neil Armstrong was the first person to walk on the moon. Such innovators reflect the progressive nature of their native state. Ohio offered its citizens such amenities as the first free home mail delivery, the first unemployment compensation program, and, after years of overgrazing, over-developing, and environmental pollution and erosion, the first nature conservancy district, which has served as a model for federal legislation.

No one is quite sure who Ohio's first inhabitants were. Mounds built by these people are scattered throughout the state's southern and central landscapes, but the mounds often spark more questions

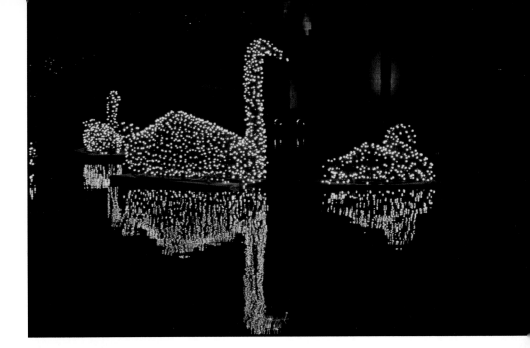

Top to bottom: At holiday time, the "sexy" Cincinnati Zoo breeds light animals as well as real ones. Overlooks scattered throughout Eden Park, at the top of one of Cincinnati's seven hills, provide magnificent views of the Ohio River. Within the park are the Cincinnati Art Museum, the Playhouse in the Park, the Cincinnati Historical Society, the Cincinnati Museum of Natural History, and Krohn Conservatory, boasting 1,500 labeled specimens of tropical plants and seasonal floral displays.

Above: It's water that runs through the veins of this city: The spirit of Cincinnati is immortalized in the *Spirit of America*, a side-wheeler with a nonwagering casino, dance hall, saloon, and café at Covington Landing, RiverCenter. *Below:* Built along the Ohio River in 1988 to commemorate Cincinnati's bicentennial, the Commons at Sawyer Point (left) encompass 22 acres of promenades, gardens, and overlooks that merge effortlessly into the next park, Yeatman's Cove (right). This is the site where the original two dozen settlers landed their flatboats and built log cabins in 1788.

This page: Riverboats, which first brought prosperity to Cincinnati, now carry people instead of merchandise. The *Delta Queen,* an overnight paddlewheel, is probably the most famous, but a variety of other riverboats feature sightseeing and romantic evening cruises. *Overleaf:* The first major city west of the Alleghenies, Cincinnati has been known as the "Queen City of the West" since the 1800's, when Henry Wadsworth Longfellow paid tribute to it in his poem "Catawaba Wine."

than they answer. The Great Serpent Mound, in southeastern Ohio, is one of the country's most intriguing enigmas: Nearly a quarter-mile long, it resembles a snake uncoiling. An oval embankment at one end may be the open mouth of the serpent as it strikes, or possibly an egg that the snake is swallowing. The largest snake effigy in North America, historians speculate that the mound was built approximately 2,500 years ago for religious or mystical purposes. Although some say it was constructed by the Adena Indians, it was not built over burials or the remnants of any living areas, so there were no artifacts found in it to identify its culture.

Just north of the Serpent Mound is Fort Hill, what appears to be an ancient fort surrounded by earth and stone, possibly built by the Hopewell tribe. The Hopewell are also responsible for the 23 burial mounds found farther north, near Chillicothe, in the 13 acres that make up Mound City. Although much of the area was destroyed by military training during World War I, many of the mounds can still be seen, and a museum houses various decorated vessels, pipes, beads, and fossils that were found in the mounds.

The oldest building in Ohio, the Company Land Office (1788), is also in the southern part of the state, in Marietta.

Top: Although a thriving commercial center now, Dayton's early industry was rocked by repeated flooding. A disastrous flood in 1913 provided the impetus for developing the Miami Conservancy District, allowing for the construction of a dam flood-control system and paving the way for passage of the National Conservancy Act. *Left:* Spectacular year round, the 70-foot-high glass dome skylight of Dayton's Arcade Square really shines when decorated for Christmas.

Downtown Dayton's only surviving theater, the 1865 Victoria Theatre, has been completely renovated and once again hosts a variety of live shows. *Below:* Modeled after a sixteenth-century villa, the exterior of the Dayton Art Institute is as much a masterpiece as the treasures within.

The Carillon Historical Park depicts the history of the Miami Valley from 1796, when the first white settlers came to the area, to the early twentieth century. *Below:* Set on a 100-foot bluff overlooking the Great Miami River, the Miamisburg Mound is one of the largest conical mounds in the northeastern United States. *Opposite:* Completed in 1850, this Greek Revival limestone building served as the county courthouse until 1884. Now called the Old Courthouse Museum, it focuses on local history, including exhibits on the National Cash Register Company, started by Dayton native John Patterson after he purchased the rights to James Ritty's patented cash register.

The birthplace of Orville and Wilbur Wright, Dayton has become synonymous with aviation. The city hosts the Dayton Air Show, one of the largest in the country, which features exhibits such as the Wright "B" military flyer (above) and flying acts from around the world. *Opposite:* The oldest and largest military aviation museum in the world, the United States Air Force Museum in Dayton is also the most popular free attraction in Ohio. The museum chronicles the history of flight from the first experiments of the Wright brothers to Space-Age Boeing missiles.

In 1788, a group of Revolutionary War veterans traded in their Continental Army IOUs for 1.5 million acres in Ohio. They went down the Ohio River in flatboats to the point where it met the Muskingum River and founded Marietta, the first permanent American settlement in the Northwest Territory. Surprisingly, the city hasn't changed much since then – it's too far off the beaten track for the twentieth century to pay it much attention. On the original site of Campus Martius, the seat of government for the Northwest Territory from 1788 to 1790, is a museum with exhibits of the early government and settlers as well as Native American crafts and costumes.

Slightly north of Marietta is Clarington and the beginning of Route 78, called the "rim of the world" by locals. Motorists who have followed the road all the way west to Nelsonville compare the experience to being in the front seat of a roller coaster.

A little farther west is some of the most spectacular scenery in the state. The glaciers that covered most of Ohio never made it this far south, so there is a greater variety of terrain than in the other, flatter, parts of the state.

Toledo pays tribute with the Martin Luther King Memorial Bridge and its sculpture "Radiance"–three faces of the great leader looking off in different directions (top). At the end of the bridge is the impressive black glass headquarters building of the glass company Owens Illinois. Its grounds include "Propylaea" (left), designed by sculptor Dimitri Hadzi to highlight Toledo's role as a gateway to the sea.

Above: As one of the largest ports on the Great Lakes, Toledo takes great pride in the boat docks, brick-lined walkways, and fluttering flags of its revitalized downtown riverfront area. *Below:* A fine example of Collegiate Gothic architecture, University Hall (left) is the center point of the University of Toledo. Founded in 1872, the school's mission was to train young people for practical tasks. A statue in Hood Park (right) on the Maumee River commemorates the soldiers and sailors of Perrysburg Township. Until the Treaty of Green Ville was signed in 1795, there were frequent confrontations between the settlers and Native Americans.

Hocking Hills State Park has some of the most unusual views, with six major rock formations within hiking distance of each other. Old Man's Cave, named after the hermit who spent the last years of his life there, is full of tunnels and stairways leading off in all directions; at the end of the gorge is Old Man's Creek, which falls 40 feet into a catch pool. Also worthy of note are Ash Cave, a sandstone overhang with a waterfall that drops about 90 feet into a small pool, and the colorfully named Pulpit Rock, Devil's Bathtub, and Conkle's Hollow (no one knows who Conkle was, but he claimed the area by inscribing his name and the year 1797 in the gorge).

To the southwest is the town of Ripley, where the Reverend John Rankin kept a lantern in the window of his house during the Civil War as a symbol of welcome to slaves crossing the Ohio River from Kentucky. It is said that the Rankin House is where Harriet Beecher Stowe first heard the story of Eliza crossing the ice—a tale later recounted in her famous novel *Uncle Tom's Cabin*.

Preceding page: The oldest lighthouse on Lake Erie, the Marblehead Lighthouse still serves as a beacon for sailors around the tip of Marblehead Peninsula. *This page:* The Lake Erie Islands are only a ferry ride away from the mainland. The rough waters around Marblehead Peninsula (top) belie the picturesque orchards and vineyards of its interior. Kelleys Island (right) boasts one of the world's largest examples of glacial grooves—400 feet of limestone bedrock scored by glaciers carrying stones millions of years ago.

Limestone quarrying, wine production, and log milling have been replaced by tourism as the primary industry on Kelleys Island. The largest American island on Lake Erie, Kelleys is one of the few islands to be named in its entirety as a National Historic District.

The Greek Revival house where Stowe lived as a young woman is in Cincinnati. Located midpoint on the Ohio River, the city of Cincinnati was another important stop on what was known as the Underground Railroad. Mt. Adams, with its Victorian bungalows, bistros, and steep, narrow streets, provides one of the best views of the "Queen City." From this vantage point, it's not hard to see why Winston Churchill dubbed Cincinnati "the most beautiful inland city in America."

One of the city's numerous bridges, the Suspension Bridge, was the first to span the Ohio River, in 1867. Built by John Augustus Roebling, it is considered the prototype for his Brooklyn Bridge. Two years later, the Cincinnati Red Stockings became the first all-professional baseball team in the United States—and won all 64 games they played that year.

In addition to being known for soap (Procter & Gamble is headquartered there), museums, and orchestras, Cincinnati has the distinction of being home to what *Newsweek* called the sexiest zoo in the country. The second-oldest zoo in the United States, it's a leader in successfully breeding animals and has one of the best groups of big cats in the world, including white tigers, King cheetahs (with stripes instead of spots),

With 54 rides, Cedar Point, on the banks of Lake Erie near Sandusky, is the largest ride park in the United States. Adventure-seekers thrill to the park's 10 roller coasters, especially The Magnum—named in the *Guinness Book of Records* both as being the fastest coaster in the world and having the longest drop.

and rare Bengal tigers, as well as the world's smallest cat. A possibly even scarier kind of animal can be found to the north at the amusement park King's Island. At 7,400 feet, "The Beast" is the longest wooden roller coaster in the world.

There must be something in the air around this part of the country that gives natives the impetus to explore the wild blue yonder. Although their famous first flight took place at Kitty Hawk, in North Carolina, the Wright brothers did their first experiments in their hometown of Dayton, where they later returned to perfect their craft. The city certainly hasn't forgotten the brothers or their contributions: The Wright Brothers Bicycle Shop is now an exhibit hall with early aviation artifacts; visitors still place wreaths at the Wright Brothers Memorial every December 17th to commemorate their first flight in 1903; and the Wright Patterson Air Force Base, just outside the city, is home to the United States Air Force Museum, with exhibits that tell the story of aviation—from the brothers' experiments all the way through to the Space Age. Even their sister, Katharine Wright, is honored at the International Women's Air & Space Museum, along with other women important to aviation, such as Amelia Earhart and Sally Ride.

This Victorian house in Fremont (top), built in 1873, was large enough to be a comfortable home to Charles and Ann Dillon and their eight children. The family were the first neighbors of Rutherford B. Hayes, who lived across the street at Spiegel Grove before and after he was the 19th president. Hayes is buried on the estate grounds (left), and the 1859 mansion is now a museum featuring a presidential library that holds more than one million manuscripts and 75,000 photographs.

Before the turn of the century, wine-making was one of the primary industries in the Lake Erie region. Wineries such as Mon Ami on Catawaba Island (above) and the Engels & Krudwig Wine Company on Water Street in Sandusky (below) today combine state-of-the-art techniques with time-tested traditions.

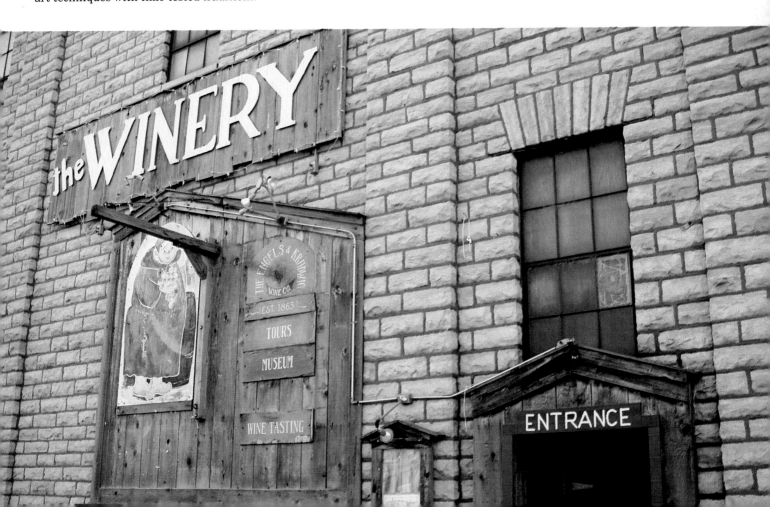

Settlers from Connecticut carved out the town of Sandusky in the early nineteenth century, using brick and locally quarried limestone. The result was the largest collection of limestone buildings in Ohio, representing every conceivable Victorian style. Many of the commercial buildings lining Water Street (above, and below, left), one block from the bay, are still in use. From the Cedar Point Building in Sandusky (below, right), ferries set out frequently during the day for the 15-minute trip to Cedar Point Amusement Park.

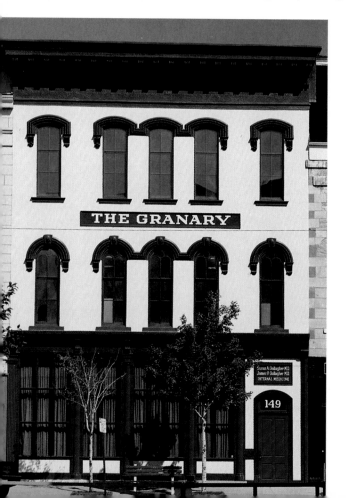

The little brick house in Milan where Thomas Edison first saw the light of day is now a museum featuring family belongings. An adjacent building houses memorabilia and early models of some of his inventions. *Below:* The Mad River and NKP Railroad Society Museum, in Bellevue, provides a hands-on look at the nation's rail system with restored passenger and freight cars, engines, and an authentic train depot. *Overleaf:* Looking at the clean and peaceful Cuyahoga River now, it's hard to believe that in 1969 it was so polluted it actually caught fire. City officials and private industry pulled together to clean up the river and jump start Cleveland's revitalization.

A renovated warehouse district with nightclubs, restaurants, stores, and a waterfront boardwalk, The Flats takes its name from the flat land on both banks of the Cuyahoga River. At night, fun-loving Clevelanders jam the river with boats, and water taxis do a brisk business. *Opposite:* The Cuyahoga County Soldiers and Sailors Monument, commemorating men who served in the Civil War, is a focal point of Cleveland's 10-acre Public Square. In the background rises the BP America Building, formerly the headquarters of the Standard Oil Company, started in 1870 by John D. Rockefeller—who eventually became the nation's first billionaire.

A friend of the Wright brothers, Paul Laurence Dunbar, was famous in his own right – before them, in fact. The Dayton home where the son of ex-slaves wrote more than 100 novels, short stories, and poems, is now a state memorial.

West of Dayton, near the Indiana border, is Oxford, home of Miami University ("the prettiest campus that ever was," according to Robert Frost) and another important writer, William McGuffey. The house where he wrote the famous McGuffey Readers series – responsible for teaching generations of young readers such important lessons as "Waste not, want not," "Look before you leap," and "Where there's a will, there's a way" – is now a National Historic Landmark and museum.

Nearby is the Miamisburg Mound, one of the largest conical mounds in the northeastern United States. Built by the Adena, with burials at several levels, the mound covers one-and-one-half acres at its base and rises 65 feet high.

To the north is an area of rolling plains and forests. While other regions in Ohio were being settled, the northwest, bordered by Michigan, Indiana, and the tip of Lake Erie, continued to be occupied by Native Americans who did not want to give up their land.

Preceding page: The Cleveland Art Museum is known as one of the finest in the country. With a free admission policy, it is also one of the most accessible. *This page, top:* Art Deco statues representing different forms of transportation line the Hope Memorial Bridge, which links downtown with Ohio City, one of Cleveland's oldest neighborhoods. *Right:* The Cleveland Museum of Natural History is a leader in putting together the pieces of the prehistoric jigsaw puzzle. Founded in 1920, the museum immortalizes dinosaur fossils, prehistoric creatures, and Lucy – the oldest and most complete fossil of a human ancestor.

Early settlers were just as happy not to venture into the dark, wet forests called the "Black Swamp" on early maps. It wasn't until the mid-nineteenth century that people started to settle in the area—mostly Germans and Poles brought in to work on the canals that eventually made the region more habitable.

Toledo, at the mouth of the Maumee River, is the only big city in this part of the state, and it took a while for it to achieve that status. In the late eighteenth century there was some settlement in the area, but it was abandoned during the War of 1812. It was re-settled in 1837 after the year-long Toledo War, when Ohio and Michigan fought over the rights to the region.

To the south and west of Toledo is Oak Openings; the name dates back to the time when clearings in the area were more unusual than the forests surrounding them. Although the lake shore is nowhere near the region now, sand dunes remain as testimony of what once was.

More sand can be found to the north on any of the Lake Erie Islands, a chain of about 20 islands. The largest, Kelley's Island, is popular with tourists who come to see Inscription Rock, decorated with picto-graphs carved by Native Americans long ago, and vin-tage homes built in the less

Whatever you're looking for, Cleveland's got a market for it. The glass-enclosed Galleria and Towers at Erieview (top) was downtown's first upscale retail complex, completed in 1987. For a taste of the Old World, the 100 food merchants at the West Side Market (center) serve up a delicious sampling of Cleveland's ethnic cuisines. Holiday lights at the Cleveland Arcade (bottom) sparkle all the more brilliantly with glass sky-lights, marble staircases, and brass railings as a backdrop.

Neat historic row houses, such as these along Prospect Avenue, are tucked into pockets throughout Cleveland. *Below:* Case Western Reserve University is just one of 70 cultural, educational, health-care, and religious institutions in Cleveland's square-mile University Circle.

Preceding page: The stone-and-stucco Kirtland Temple was the first permanent church built by followers of Mormon leader Joseph Smith. Parishioners who had migrated from New York and Pennsylvania completed the church in 1836, just six years after the Church of Latter Day Saints was organized in New York. *This page:* Northeastern Ohio is still referred to as the Western Reserve, dating from the nineteenth century, when Ohio was considered "the West." Small towns share the New England feel they inherited from Connecticut settlers, while maintaining their own identity. Old-fashioned Chardon (above left) attracts visitors from all over with its annual maple sugar festival. Wellington, once part of the Underground Railroad, comes to life with colorful Victorian houses (center) and a Gothic town hall (right). The falls from which Chagrin Falls took its name run right under Main Street (below).

Although the waves still crash against Fairport
Harbor, the once thriving nineteenth-century
port on Lake Erie has become a quiet community.
The lighthouse, built in 1871, is now a museum
featuring navigational instruments, marine
charts, a pilothouse from a Great Lakes ship—
and a great view of the lake shore.

distant past. The entire island is on the National Register of Historic Places. South Bass Island, once a playground for presidents and millionaires, is still the most popular of the islands, primarily for the view from the top of the town Put-in-Bay. Middle Bass is best known for Lonz Winery, which looks like a medieval castle and can be toured from mid-May through late September. Back on the mainland is the Marblehead Lighthouse on Marblehead Peninsula. Built in 1821, it's the oldest lighthouse on the Great Lakes and is still operating.

The peninsula is only one locale in northern Ohio that features acres of picturesque vineyards and orchards. This is one of the regions traversed in the early 1800's by John Chapman, who was later immortalized as Johnny Appleseed. According to legend, Chapman came to Ohio without any shoes and wearing a sack as a shirt. He owned an apple orchard near Mansfield and was known for planting apple seeds wherever he went. To this day, apple festivals featuring such homemade specialties as apple cider and apple butter are popular throughout the state. Mixed in with the farms and wineries of northeastern Ohio are larger industrialized cities and charming small

The last president born in a log cabin, James A. Garfield conducted his first successful "front porch" campaign for the presidency from Lawnfield, his Victorian home in Mentor. He was assassinated shortly after his inauguration in 1881 by a disappointed office-seeker.

Wind surfing is a common pastime at Headlands Beach State Park, on Lake Erie near Mentor.

The lush Mill Creek Park is a tranquil oasis running right through the middle of Youngstown. Its 2,500 acres include a covered bridge (above); the restored grist mill, Lanterman's Mill (below); three lakes; formal gardens; and 36 holes of golf.

towns still bearing a strong New England influence. As recently as 200 years ago, this part of the state was considered part of the American West; the area is still referred to as the Western Reserve, land originally claimed by the state of Connecticut.

Cleveland, calling itself "The Comeback City," is a prime example of the state's need to be progressive. Founded in 1796, the story has it the city got its name when a newspaper inadvertently left the "a" out of founder Moses Cleaveland's name. Providing heavy industry used by the North for the war effort, Cleveland's growth took off during the Civil War and continued with entrepreneurs such as John D. Rockefeller, the nation's first billionaire, who started the Standard Oil Company in 1870.

Cleveland became one of the nation's leading steelmaking cities, but by 1969 it had gone too far. That was the year the Cuyahoga River, which runs through the city, was so polluted that it actually caught fire. Backed by an unusual cooperation between private industry and government, Cleveland set about revitalizing: Today "The Flats," once a warehouse district on both sides of the Cuyahoga, is a lively symbol of Cleveland's regeneration with shops, restaurants, and clubs. Clevelanders also point with pride to

Top: Although steel-making in Youngstown dropped off steeply in the late 1970's, some mills remain in business. *Right:* A chronicle of the industry's history is told at the Youngstown Historical Center of Industry and Labor, whose mission is to promote knowledge of the region's industrial background through exhibits and education.

Above, left: The National McKinley Birthplace Memorial was built in the city of Niles 14 years after William McKinley was assassinated in 1901. This statue depicts the way the 25th president looked as he made his last speech. *Right:* Modeled after Yale, Western Reserve College was founded by Hudson residents in the early 1800's. The college moved to Cleveland in 1882, and the facility was taken over by the Western Reserve Academy, a private preparatory school. *Below:* Hale Farm and Village, in Bath, re-creates life as it was for Western Reserve settlers in the mid-1800's. Buildings threatened with destruction from all over the region have been moved to the village for preservation. *Opposite:* The Valley Line Railroad chugs through the Cuyahoga Valley between Akron and Cleveland with stops at Hale Farm and Quaker Square, a shopping complex created from the original Quaker Oats factory.

Akron, already the "Rubber Capital of the World," has become an internationally recognized leader in polymer research, with much of the work taking place in the Polymer Building at the University of Akron. *Below:* The outdoor Sculpture Court at the Akron Art Museum is frequently the site of concerts and special events. *Opposite:* William McKinley, the 25th president, lived nine days after being shot when shaking hands in a crowd after a speech in Buffalo, New York. He is interred in the McKinley National Memorial in Canton, a circular Beaux Arts stone mausoleum set in a 23-acre park.

Above: Unlike some of the other nineteenth-century industrial cities, Canton retains its steel industry as a big business. *Below, left:* The birthplace of professional football in 1920, Canton scored again when it became the home of the Professional Football Hall of Fame. The four-building complex features memorabilia and two enshrinement halls, as well as a theater, research library, and gift shop. *Right:* Crowning the Stark County Courthouse in Canton, "Heralds of Justice" serves as a constant reminder of the court's mission. A frieze depicting agriculture, commerce, justice, and industry decorates a portico below the tower.

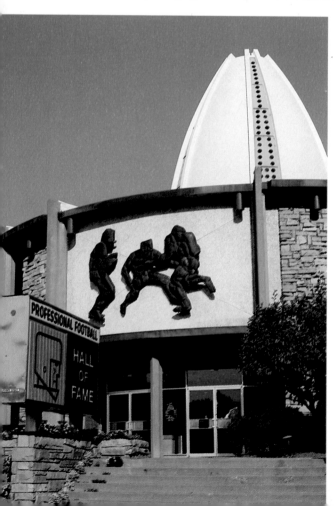

University Circle. Within a single square mile, the circle holds one of the largest concentrations of culture found anywhere, including the Cleveland Museum of Art (ranked as one of the top five art museums in the country) and Severance Hall, home of the Cleveland Orchestra, known as one of the world's finest. And nothing can beat the smile on a Clevelander's face when he or she tells you Cleveland—whose native son Alan Freed coined the phrase "rock 'n' roll"—is soon to become home to the Rock 'N' Roll Hall of Fame.

While the state is committed to cleaning up wrongs from the past, it is also dedicated to preserving history. On the way south to Akron from Cleveland is Hale Farm, in Bath, a re-created town that depicts life from 1800 to 1850. Akron, the biggest rubber-making city in the country, is home to the Stan Hywet Hall, the largest private residence in Ohio, a Tudor Revival home built by profits from rubber. Just south is Canton, sporting the Pro Football Hall of Fame.

Moving southwest towards central Ohio, first-time visitors may be puzzled by road signs warning of slow-moving horse-drawn vehicles. This is Amish Country, in Holmes, Wayne, and Tuscarawas counties, where

In 1817, German separatists seeking religious freedom formed Zoar Village in Tuscarawas County. There they maintained a communal society until 1898, when members divided the common property and dissolved the community. The more significant buildings are operated by the Ohio Historical Society as museums; others have become shops and bed-and-breakfasts. In 1960, the tinsmith's shop (bottom) was reconstructed on its original site, using the Zoarite technique "nogging," in which brick is placed between reinforcing framing timbers.

the people live much the way they did when they first settled here at the beginning of the nineteenth century. You won't find automobiles, electricity, or telephones, but you will find meadows, farms, and pastures, as well as some of the best fresh ham, breads, and peanut butter pie. Another interesting mix of the old and the new can be found in Newark at the Moundbuilders State Memorial. The great ceremonial circle was originally built by the Hopewell; about 2,000 years later, it was the site of the first Ohio state fair. Nearby is the 138-acre Octagon State Memorial, an ancient preserved circle and octagon mounds tied together—and a modern private golf course.

Few people know it, but nearby Homer is birthplace to Victoria Claflin Woodhull, who in 1872 became the first woman candidate for president. Another Ohioan, Ulysses S. Grant, beat her in the race, but she did become a local legend for the effort. A better-known look at the past can be had at the Robbins Hunter Museum, a 27-room mansion in Granville, which the Smithsonian calls one of the two best examples of Greek Revival interiors in America.

Columbus, the state capital, also boasts fine architecture, particularly the State Capitol, which is considered one of the nation's purest examples of Doric architecture. When choosing the capital city in 1816, one

About 35,000 Amish people live in Ohio. A horse-and-buggy (top) remains the preferred mode of transportation, and fields are farmed (left) by tried-and-true methods, without modern machinery. *Opposite:* Bonnets top off the outfits of the typical Amish schoolgirl. Amish children often end their formal education after the upper elementary school grades.

The Harding Memorial in Marion honors the last president to hail from Ohio, Warren G. Harding. Although the newspaper owner claimed he didn't want to run—and stayed at home in Marion during the campaign—he was elected the 29th president; he died in office in 1923.

Above: Roscoe Village (left) in Coshocton County re-creates an early nineteenth-century canal town in the days before railroads, when canals were the lifeblood of commerce and industry. Across the Walhonding River is the city of Coshocton, site of the county courthouse (right). *Below:* Visitors can take a ride on the *Monticello III,* a replica of a horse-drawn canal boat that regularly leaves from Roscoe Village and runs on a restored section of the Ohio and Erie Canal.

Above: An Italianate farmhouse built in 1867, Daweswood House Museum is on the grounds of the 1,000-plus-acre Dawes Arboretum, in Newark. It is said that oilman Beman Davis bought the property to prevent lumbermen from cutting down its trees. *Below, left:* Set in the middle of a large town square, Licking County Courthouse, in Newark, boasts frescoed ceilings, elaborate light fixtures, and hardwood walls. *Right:* The bottom part of the Muskingum County Courthouse, built in 1809, briefly enjoyed status as statehouse from 1810 to 1812, when Zanesville was state capital. The top section, seen here, was added in 1870.

of the committee's stipulations was that it be "not more than 40 miles from the common center of the State." This eliminated the then-capital of Zanesville, as well as the previous capital of Chillicothe, both of which fell just outside this boundary. A group of businessmen got together and offered to lay out a town on the east bank of the Scioto River, at the time an unnamed forested area. The legislature accepted and later chose the name Columbus, which eventually grew to be the largest of the many cities worldwide named after Christopher Columbus.

Columbus likes to do things big. The largest city in Ohio, it is home to Ohio State University, the largest college campus in North America; the nation's largest state fair, which runs for 18 days every August; and Battell Memorial Institute, the world's largest private research facility.

The people of Columbus—and the whole state of Ohio—epitomize what the United States stands for, constantly striving to make life easier and better. From an undeveloped land of lakes, forests, and plains, they have managed to sculpt some of our finest cities, farms, universities, and cultural centers. Yet they are always mindful of preserving and learning from the past. Ohio truly is America's heartland.

The frame Sherman House (top) is the boyhood home of brothers General William Tecumseh Sherman, responsible for the burning of Atlanta during the Civil War, and Senator John Sherman, author of the 1890 Sherman Antitrust Act. This house is just one example of the many kinds of nineteenth-century architecture preserved in Lancaster's historic Square 13 (center). This red brick townhouse (bottom), called The Georgian, is a particularly fine example of the Georgian architectural style employed in the middle colonies and mid-Atlantic states.

Preceding page: Canyons, cliffs, gorges, caves, and forest weave a lush tapestry through Hocking Hills State Park. Near Old Man's Cave, Upper Falls runs down in a string of waterfalls before plunging under a bridge and continuing with another series of small falls that lead to the final grand drop of Lower Falls. *This page:* Built of stone and yellow clay, the Great Serpent Mound uncoils for almost a quarter of a mile through southwestern Ohio. Archaeologists are still trying to unravel the mystery of who constructed the serpent effigy 2,500 years ago— and why.

Preceding pages: Across the Scioto (pronounced "sye-otto") River, the Columbus skyline rises majestically from the flat plains of central Ohio. *This page:* Columbus takes an active interest in promoting the arts. Ralph Helmick's 11-foot-high sculpture of Wyandot Indian chief Leatherlips, in Scioto Park (above), is the result of a national art competition sponsored by the city. The postmodern Wexner Center for the Arts at Ohio State University (below) draws international acclaim for its exhibitions, media arts, and performing arts and education.

Above: The largest city in Ohio, the state capital is also the largest city in the world named after Christopher Columbus. *Below, left:* City officials take care of business in City Hall, while the state legislature meets in the Statehouse, a neoclassical building marked by its lack of dome. *Right:* On its grounds, "These Are My Jewels" is the sentiment expressed by the woman atop this statue, describing the Civil War–era soldiers in a circle below her.

Preceding page: All that remains today of Columbus's Camp Chase, the largest Confederate prison in the North during the Civil War, is a cemetery containing the graves of 2,200 Confederate soldiers who died in the prison. *This page, above:* Ohio State University claims the largest campus in North America. During weekends in the fall, football fans flock to see the Buckeyes in action. *Below, left:* Housed in a one-time arsenal, the Columbus Cultural Arts Center now proceeds more peacefully with art exhibits, lectures, concerts, and poetry readings. *Right:* It's back to the Old World in Columbus's nineteenth-century German Village. A National Historic District, its brick streets are lined with restored houses, quirky shops, ethnic restaurants, and beer gardens that add to the year-round Oktoberfest-style atmosphere.

Index of Photography

TIB indicates The Image Bank

All photographs courtesy of Image Finders where indicated *.